The Color of Hope

Transformative Power of Hope

Eric Bob

direct or indirect damages caused by the use of this material, including mistakes, omissions, or inaccuracies.

Table of Content

Introduction

Emma was a young artist who formerly resided in a sleepy little village. However, she had a talent for painting. Lately, her works have portrayed a sense of hopelessness and despair. Her once-vibrant brushstrokes had become monochromatic, reflecting the heart's increasing pessimism.

Emma came across an abandoned art studio hidden in an alley one day while strolling through the congested streets of her neighborhood. The studio was in a state of decay, with dust and cobwebs covering its windows. The area, though, seemed to have a mysterious atmosphere about it that was waiting to be uncovered.

Emma was curious, so she decided to go inside. She found a worn notebook belonging to a well-known artist called Alice Turner among the abandoned paintings and discarded brushes. Emma was drawn to the author's writing as she read through the book because she felt Alice's challenges and victories were paralleled in her life.

A tale of tenacity, hope, and the transformational power of art was revealed in Alice's notebook. She had spent a difficult period of her life in the studio, utilizing her artwork to instill optimism in a dejected neighborhood. Her creations had developed into a source of illumination that inspired hope in those who saw them.

Each page Emma read increased her interest. She sought out the elderly residents of the area who had known the artist in an effort to learn more about the artist's legacy. As they recalled Alice's persistent faith in art's therapeutic and uplifting potential, their eyes sparkled with happy recollections.

Emma discovered a secret painting in the studio because she was curious. Alice's unfinished masterpiece was a stunning portrayal of a colorful and intriguing universe that danced across the canvas. When Emma recognized that this painting contained the secret to her own path to hope, her heart began to beat faster with eagerness.

Emma set off on a mission to finish Alice's masterpiece and infuse it with her vision of hope, driven by her newly discovered purpose. With each stroke, she echoed the feelings that had lain dormant inside her by blending vibrant red, tranquil blue and vivid yellow hues.

The town was inundated with news of Emma's mission like wildfire. Her tenacity captured people's attention, and the charm in her paintings moved them. They contributed their tales of optimism, fortitude, and triumph over hardship, which helped to amplify Emma's motivation.

Emma decided to put together an art exhibition with the working title "The Color of Hope" to spread the transformational power of art. Her paintings would be on display, but the exhibition would also provide a forum for the inspirational tales that the neighborhood had produced.

The exhibition's preparation was with its difficulties. Emma began to experience self-doubt and anxiety, which threatened to extinguish the sputtering glimmer of optimism she had sparked. She persisted still, relying on the fortitude Alice had taught in her.

The art center was buzzing with anticipation as the day of the exhibition approached. People's eyes opened in amazement as they entered the gallery due to the vibrant colors decorating the walls. Emma's artwork triggered feelings that had been long buried.

Chapter 1

The Artist Emma

Emma was a young artist who formerly resided in a tiny town surrounded by lush meadows and rolling hills. Thanks to her vivacious spirit and deft fingers, she had always sought comfort in the world of colors and brushstrokes. People may be transported to enchanted worlds by her paintings, which also have the potential to stir up intense emotions.

Emma, however, discovered herself trapped in a never-ending misery as the years went by. The vibrant colors that formerly decorated her canvases had faded into subdued gray tones. Her creative spirit had been enveloped in a shroud of hopelessness that had put out the flame that had once ignited her heart.

The once-vibrant and inspiring Emma's art studio now resembled a forlorn haven. Her formerly vibrant environment was thrown in shadow as the smell of dried paint combined with the weight of disappointment. She would sit in front of a blank canvas daily, her hands shaking with annoyance as she tried vainly to awaken her sleeping creativity.

Her soul yearned for a way out of this never-ending circle of gloom. To rekindle her creative fire, Emma took solace in taking long strolls through the town's winding streets. She was wandering through a busy market square one bright day when she noticed a worn signpost pointing toward a neglected alley.

Emma was intrigued and followed the hint, arriving at an old door in front of a time-frozen art studio. She opened the rusted doorknob with shaking hands and entered a world that had not changed through the years.

The studio was alive with the echoes of creative aspirations inside. The dust-covered windows let in rays of sunlight that reflected off the worn wooden floor, creating mystical patterns. Unfinished and abandoned canvases leaned against the walls, whispering tales of unfulfilled dreams.

Emma walked around the room, her fingers brushing across the delicate strokes of works of art that had been left behind and each of which still contained a piece of the artist's heart. She found a battered leather-bound journal hidden under a stack of rejected sketches in the corner.

She carefully read the journal's pages out of curiosity, revealing the private thoughts of its previous owner, an artist by the name of Alice Turner. Emma watched as Alice's words danced before her, describing a life devoted to the pursuit of art and the beauty it contained.

In her works, Alice expressed a firm confidence in the ability of creativity to change people for the better and in the capacity of art to enlighten the deepest recesses of the human psyche. Emma identified with this historical artist since their difficulties resembled the brushstrokes of a masterpiece.

Emma was drawn into Alice's book by a new sense of purpose, finding inspiration in the accounts of her victories and her unflinching resiliency in the face of hardship. She ate up stories of Alice's interactions with other artists, their camaraderie lighting a spark of hope in her worn-out heart.

Emma's once-dulled palette started to spark with the faintest trace of color as each page turned. A faint impulse urged her to pick up her paintbrushes again and reawaken her dormant artistic talent.

Emma searched the town's older residents who had known the artist while in her prime because she was eager to learn more about Alice's world. As they discussed Alice's art displays, where her paintings had served as rays of hope during dark times, their eyes sparkled with recollections. Through their personal stories, Emma started to understand art's influence on a neighborhood and how it might bring people together and spark hope.

Emma set off on a voyage of self-discovery armed with Alice's notebook and the collective recollections of the town's residents. In the middle of the city, beneath the protection of a massive oak tree, she set up an easel and started painting. With each stroke, she poured her need, her yearning, and her wish for hope onto the canvas.

The villagers saw Emma had changed. They saw as her once-gray paintings started to have a vibrancy that resembled the flowering plants in the meadows. The vivid color whirls, minute details, and the emotions that seemed to burst off the canvases astounded them.

Emma's makeover became widely known. People came from all around because of their curiosity to see an artist awakened and be moved by the enchantment emanating from her works. Emma's artwork became a refuge and a source of motivation for individuals who had lost their capacity for fantasy.

Emma put together an exhibition to pay tribute to Alice's legacy and her reignited spirit after accepting her role as a harbinger of hope. The goal of the exhibition, titled "The Color of Hope," was to bring the town's creatives together under one roof to celebrate the beauty that art might bring to their lives.

The excitement in the air grew as the exhibition day approached. The vivid paintings by Emma that decorated the gallery walls turned them into a tapestry of dreams, with each stroke demonstrating the strength of hope. Visitors' eyes were filled with delight as they absorbed the histories behind each painting as they explored the area.

Emma stood in the middle of the show, surrounded by other artists, her pulse throbbing in time with theirs. She observed the happy tears, the giggling that danced on lips, and the spark of inspiration reflected in everyone who gazed upon her work. She understood then that her travel had not been for nothing.

In addition to Emma's life, "The Color of Hope" also changed the lives of everyone present. It evolved into a tribute to the resiliency of the human spirit, a declaration that even in the most hopeless situations, there is always a reason for optimism in an artist's brushstrokes or the melody of a song.

From that moment on, Emma's workshop transformed into a haven for creation where people sought solace, healing, and inspiration. She developed the budding artistic abilities of aspiring artists and shared Alice's knowledge and the collective hope stories.

The ebb and flow of Emma's personal emotions were reflected in her art as it continued to develop. She addressed the broad spectrum of optimism in her paintings, including the soft resiliency of a blooming flower, the serene consolation of a pastel sunset, and the powerful resolve of a flaming daybreak.

As a result, Emma's tale was woven into the fabric of her community and stands as a tribute to the ability of hope to transform lives and the unyielding spirit of an artist. She became a beacon of hope for others who had lost their way, as a gentle reminder that even in the darkest times, there are always shades of hope ready to paint their lives magically.

Emma Comes Across A Vintage, Abandoned Art Studio.

Emma had a sharp eye for beauty and a heart that yearned to use her work to reveal the depths of her imagination. Her inventiveness had, however, recently been dwindling, and a gloomy emptiness had enveloped her vivacious soul.

While strolling around the well-known streets one fall afternoon, Emma saw a neglected neighborhood area. It was an odd location that had always seemed to be disregarded as if it were keeping something from the public. Emma was lured to an ancient, abandoned building isolated among overgrown vines and flaking paint due to her heightened curiosity.

The structure was a long-abandoned and neglected art studio. It exuded a sense of mystery and sorrow as if its worn walls contained the echoes of lost hopes and untold tales. Years of disrepair, they had smeared the glass, creating a sinister shadow in the vicinity.

Emma pulled open the squeaky door and entered a world trapped in time because she was intrigued by the studio's mysterious vibe. Old paint odor overpowered her senses, merging with the heaviness of the airborne perfume of memories.

An ethereal aura was produced by dust particles dancing in the beams of sunshine that peaked through the roof's fissures.

Emma's eyes expanded in astonishment and pleasure as she entered the studio deeper. Layers of dust and cobwebs adhered to the canvasses placed carelessly against the walls. Worn-out and ragged brushes were strewn about on tables covered in paint splatter. Each brushstroke was preserved in time and wrapped in the remains of art.

Emma delicately removed a dusty painting from its resting place, unable to resist the pull of the abandoned works of art. A flash of color—a window into the past—emerged as she used her hands to remove the layers of neglect. A vibrant cityscape was shown in the artwork, yet there was also a tinge of melancholy weaved throughout the brushstrokes. It appeared as though the artist had poured their heart and soul into the painting, leaving something behind.

Emma's exploration was driven by curiosity as she uncovered more lost works of art, each one containing its own narrative and feelings. The studio had evolved into a time capsule containing the hopes and ambitions of long-gone artists. It was as though their presence lingered in the air she inhaled, whispering tales of victory and anguish.

Emma found an old leather-bound journal in the far corner of the studio. She thought it was calling to her as if the words inside would help her unlock the secrets of the work and the studio itself. She turned the pages with shaky hands, revealing the innermost feelings and encounters of the artists who had formerly resided here.

The journal's writer was a well-known painter named Amelia, who had made the studio her haven. Amelia let Emma see into her soul with the tenderness of her words. She documented her creative process, including the peaks of inspiration and the valleys of self-doubt. Emma was particularly captivated by the enigmatic passages, which hinted at a treasure waiting to be found inside the studio.

Following the trail of clues left by Amelia's diary entries, Emma embarked on a journey, enthralled by the prospect of learning a secret. She interpreted hints concealed within the artwork in search of links and patterns that would take her farther into the heart of the studio's enigma.

As she dug deeper, Emma ran into problems and difficulties that put her resolve to the test. Paintings shifted positions when she turned her back on them, and brushes vanished without a trace, giving the studio a ghostly appearance. Nevertheless, she persevered despite each failure because she was motivated by the prospect of solving the mystery surrounding the studio.

Weeks passed into days, and Emma's life became entangled in the hunt for the lost treasure. She spent many hours dissecting paintings, searching the studio for secret storage areas, and interpreting coded notes from previous artists. It appeared she had merged with the fantastical universe in the studio and was now a part of the narrative she was trying to decipher.

A revelation hit Emma like a flash of lightning one fateful evening as she stood before a particularly alluring painting. The brushstrokes revealed a faint pattern that guided her to an area of the wall resembling the others. She put her fingers on the wall with a wave of anticipation, sensing a slight give beneath her touch.

Emma eagerly pushed up against the wall, exposing a concealed compartment. She discovered a tiny wooden box with elaborate engravings inside. As she carefully opened the box, she found a collection of letters, sketches, and a broken key, which made her heart race with anticipation.

The letters were communications between Amelia and her beloved, another artist who had inexplicably disappeared many years earlier. They discussed passion, love, and the quest for creative truth. The drawings showed fascinating settings where fantasy and reality coexisted.

But the most intriguing part was the key. It hints at closed doors and stolen goods, promising revelations that would surpass Emma's wildest expectations. Her unquenchable curiosity led her as she followed the hints in the letters and sketches to reveal long-buried mysteries in the studio.

Emma discovered treasures as she descended into the studio's secret spaces, but she also made a life-changing realization about herself. It served as a reminder that creativity can flourish amid difficulty and that inspiration can be located in the most unlikely locations. The studio had come to represent her artistic path.

After the treasure quest was over, Emma experienced a sense of rebirth. Her sanctuary, where her creativity once more bloomed, was the once-dreary studio. She repainted its walls, bringing them to life with engaging artwork and brilliant colors.

As word of Emma's discovery went around the area, the studio quickly developed into a gathering place for artists looking for comfort, motivation, and a link to the creative spirits of the past. Emma accepted her responsibility as the studio's keeper, telling its tales and inviting other artists into its intriguing embrace.

As the years went by, the studio prospered as a center for artistic expression and social interaction. Emma's creative expression flourished due to the buried riches she had found and her relationships with legendary artists. She rose to fame for her ability to express mystery and hope in her artwork, which is evidence of the studio's transforming potential.

The abandoned studio, which was formerly cloaked in mystery and neglect, has evolved into a metaphor for artistic tenacity and the continuing power of creation. Along with reigniting Emma's enthusiasm for art, Emma's trip inspired those who dared to explore the world behind its walls. The studio served as a reminder to everyone who came that there is the potential for rebirth and rejuvenation of the artistic soul, even amid the devastation. It served as a tribute to the beauty that can arise from abandoned areas.

The Lost Journal.

Meandering rivers and rolling hills surrounded a charming small village with an old, decaying art studio. This studio had a mystique, as though bygone artists' secrets were hidden beneath its deteriorating walls. Emma, a young and promising artist, would set out on a quest that would forever alter her life within this hidden realm.

Emma had always had a strong affinity for the arts. It served as her haven and refuge from the everyday realities of life. But lately, she had lost some of her creative drive and had become utterly despondent. She wished for something to rekindle her enthusiasm and give her talent some new life.

Emma noticed the antique art studio one fateful day as she strolled through her neighborhood's cobblestone alleys. She felt drawn inside by the building's deteriorated exterior and overgrown vines. She pushed open the creaky door, drawn by its eerie vibe, and entered a lost world that had been frozen in time.

The studio was alive with the specters of artistic fantasies inside. Old paint odor and dust particles danced in the golden sunlight streams that crept through the broken windows. While brushes that had been used and abandoned waited for the touch of a skillful hand, canvases that had once been vibrant and alive now lay covered in a thin layer of neglect.

Emma slowly walked around the workspace when she noticed a worn-out diary among some neglected designs. She was so curious that she leaned out to touch it. The leather cover of the journal, which had fading pages inside, said "Alice Turner" in exquisite calligraphy. Emma's pulse beat faster as she realized that those pages contained the secret tale of a former famous artist who had once graced the studio.

She opened the journal with quivering hands, exposing a world that seemed to live between the lines. Emma was captivated by Alice Turner's words, a writer whose brilliance had once shined like a beacon. In her journal, Alice described a life devoted to the creation of art, including both its joys and its sorrows.

Emma went into Alice's thoughts, her dreams, and the challenges she had to confront on page after page. The journal described artistic achievements, captivating exhibitions, and Alice's work's tremendous effect on those who saw it. However, signs of melancholy and longing mixed in with the success stories, as if Alice had a hidden desire that she was never delighted.

Emma started to feel a solid connection to the artist of the past as she became more and more absorbed in Alice's universe. She was aware of the ebbs and flows of inspiration, the frantic hunt for the elusive muse, and the tremendous influence art could have on the human soul. Emma could escape the pit of her self-doubt thanks to Alice's comments, which served as a lifeline.

Emma went deeper inside the studio, determined to discover Alice's secrets and the source of her genius as an artist. She combed through every crevice, peering behind smudged paintings and beneath heaps of misplaced sketches, looking for hints that may illuminate Alice's legacy.

As Emma painstakingly put Alice's story together, days grew into weeks. She found secret compartments on the studio's floor, which opened to disclose treasures of misplaced art materials and mementos that had special meaning for Alice. The discovery that Alice had left behind an unfinished masterwork, a picture containing the secret to her soul, was the most remarkable find.

The partially completed canvas was hidden in a corner and covered with a covering when Emma discovered it. She pulled up the cover with shaky hands, unveiling a stunning work of art that showed a world with vivid colors and otherworldly settings. Emma was drawn in by the central figure's eyes, full of longing and hope, and reflected the depths of her soul.

After discovering a new sense of purpose, Emma decided to finish Alice's masterwork independently. She immersed herself in Alice's style and the feelings that radiated from the canvas as she devoted countless hours to studying her methods. Her studio became a haven where she could communicate with Alice's soul while projecting her aspirations onto the unfinished artwork.

Emma returned to see the finished piece as the last brushstrokes were applied. It appeared as though the artwork had come to life, breathing with the hushed conversations of two creators linked by time and distance. The fact that Alice's work was finished was not only a testimonial to her brilliance but also to the tenacity of the human spirit and the ability of art to cross boundaries.

The completion of Alice's masterwork and Emma's discovery quickly became known throughout the community. The studio, which had previously been forgotten and abandoned, is now a popular destination for art enthusiasts and daydreamers. Astonished at the bond between two artists who had never met but were connected by their shared love of art, crowds of people flocked to see the beauty that radiated from within its walls.

Emma's life changed when the art studio was revived, and the legacy of Alice Turner was realized. She accepted her position as the studio's protector, telling everyone who entered its revered halls the tales of Alice and her artistic path. Just as Alice had once discovered her muse there, the studio evolved into a center for creativity where artists might seek solace and encouragement.

As a result, the abandoned journal and the artist who had given its pages life profoundly changed Emma's life. Emma regained her artistic voice while researching Alice's narrative, and her passion for art was reignited with a flame that was brighter than before. The studio evolved into a symbol of the enduring influence of art, serving as a reminder that even amid deterioration and neglect, inspiration may be discovered. And in the hands of individuals with the courage to dream, the heritage of vanished artists can be revived, paving the way and lighting a hope-filled beacon for future generations.

Alice and Emma

Emma had opened a doorway into a universe that existed outside of space and time with her exploration of the abandoned art studio and her discovery of Alice Turner's notebook. Emma was deeply moved by Alice's stories, which sparked her creative ambitions and gave her a renewed feeling of purpose.

The more Emma read through Alice's notebook, the more she realized how deeply connected the artist was to the group of people she had formerly been a part of. Those who had seen Alice's artwork through trying times found comfort and hope in its transformational potential.

Emma discovered in the notebook that Alice had produced some of her most well-known pieces during social unrest. Economic woes, political upheaval, and a general sense of hopelessness have plagued the community. In the face of these hardships, Alice's artwork had become a guiding light, giving the village's residents a glimpse of hope.

Alice's paintings' vivid colors and dynamic imagery perfectly reflected the essence of the human spirit's resiliency and the beauty that might be discovered in disaster. The locals turned to her artwork for solace, congregating at her shows to lose themselves in a realm that provided an escape from their daily problems. Her work became a symbol of fortitude, encouraging people to endure and reminding them of the natural beauty they already possessed.

Emma understood the significance of Alice's contributions to the neighborhood as she also learned how vital the art studio had been in fostering this bond. It had been a gathering place for artists and art lovers who shared a passion for creation and found consolation in the transformational power of art. The studio had served as a haven where the community's spirit had flourished despite hardship.

Emma was deeply moved by Alice's legacy and her art's enormous effect on the neighborhood, and she felt compelled to bring that spirit back to the studio. She recognized the potential for the abandoned area to blossom into a thriving center for artistic expression, where locals and artists could unite and draw courage and inspiration from one another's work.

Emma set out on a mission to bring the studio back to its former splendor with fresh vigor. She collected volunteers and local artists and told them about Alice and her art's enormous effects on the neighborhood. People from all walks of life came together to support Emma's initiative, ready to give the abandoned studio new life. The response was overwhelmingly positive.

Days progressed into weeks, and the studio changed under Emma's devoted direction. Repainted walls revealed a rainbow of hues that matched the exuberance of Alice's artwork. Fresh canvases were used instead of dusty ones and were impatiently ready to be painted. The studio's atmosphere changed, humming with a new vitality that attracted artists and fans from far and wide.

Emma organized exhibitions that featured the creations of regional artists who were as passionate about portraying the beauty of the human experience as Alice was. The displays turned into a forum for discussion, bringing the neighborhood together to celebrate and recognize the importance of art. People talked about how the visual storytelling produced by the artists had provided them with comfort, healing, and inspiration while they dealt with their problems.

The art studio evolved into a haven for those seeking solace from the stresses of daily life in addition to being a haven for artists. People were encouraged to develop their creativity and discover the hidden artist through workshops and classes. The fact that everyone was welcome at the studio helped to promote inclusivity and community.

The abandoned art studio was now alive and well, resonating with the footfall of individuals who had previously sought solace within its walls. Emma's dream had come true, and Alice's artwork had a lasting effect that touched the hearts and souls of all who entered.

As word of the renovated studio spread, it drew visitors from far-off areas who were both artists and art fans. The town gained notoriety for the studio's creative activity and the natural beauty of its surroundings. The neighborhood prospered as artists discovered a sense of community and support, encouraging cooperation and development.

Emma discovered her voice in this rich tapestry of artistic expression. Her artwork, which was influenced by Alice's story, perfectly portrayed the essence of optimism, grit, and the beauty that springs from the depths of the human soul. She carried on Alice's legacy while establishing her path, serving as a living example of art's immense impact on a person and a community.

Emma understood the power of art beyond the confines of the studio as her work impacted the hearts of those who saw it. It can comfort, uplift, and bring people together. Emma and the neighborhood had spun a tapestry of optimism through the shared experience of creativity, bringing long-forgotten dreams back to life and reigniting the enthusiasm for the arts.

The art studio thus served as a symbol of the ongoing influence of creativity and the power of art. It came to represent tenacity and serve as a reminder that beauty and optimism can be found even in the most challenging circumstances. Emma and Alice both served as catalysts for artistic expression, healing, and celebrating the human experience as their stories intertwined over time.

Emma Aims To Develop Her Sense Of Optimism.

Emma stirred within her spirit due to Alice's deep influence on the neighborhood and her artistic journey within the reopened art studio. She understood that she shared the desire to use her art to fulfill her sense of optimism and purpose. Alice's story had inspired her, and she realized she had to set out on a personal mission to find her authentic artistic voice.

Emma embarked on an adventure to explore new, literal, and metaphorical landscapes because she was curious and wanted to learn more about herself. She visited far-off locations, immersing herself in the vivid hues of the natural world, taking in the tastes and sensations of many cultures, and looking for inspiration in the variety of human experiences.

Emma traveled the world and met many artists, each with distinctive styles and viewpoints. She spoke with them, heard their tales, and absorbed their knowledge. Emma learned about the incredible ability of art to bridge linguistic and cultural divides by talking to people on a universal level of passion and creativity.

Emma felt that despite her enriching experiences, she yearned for a deeper connection that would span the chasm between her artistic vision and the mission that Alice's legacy had imbued in her. She understood that her quest involved an inside journey to discover her passions, fears, and objectives, in addition to external exploration.

Emma sank back into the comfortable embrace of the reopened art studio and started working on her project. She experimented with several mediums, pushed the envelope, and exposed herself. She poured her feelings into the painting, using them as a conduit for the optimism, tenacity, and transforming power she had seen in Alice's artwork and its effects on the neighborhood.

Emma did, however, experience self-doubt and frustration as she progressed in her artistic quest. She occasionally doubted her skills and the importance of her art, and the route she had chosen was not easy. Alice's advice resounded in her head at that precise time, reminding her that the path of an artist was not supposed to be straightforward. It was a journey of development, self-knowledge, and tenacity.

Emma's creative approach evolved into a mirror of her struggles and achievements on the inside. Every brushstroke and color selection became a metaphor for her path to optimism and meaning in life. Like Alice, she accepted her flaws and learned to see them as possibilities for improvement.

Emma's support system was the group of people who had gathered around the studio after it had been rejuvenated. She received support from other artists, art enthusiasts, and even people just looking for solace in the transformational power of art. They appreciated her dedication to her work, vulnerability, and commitment to using her art to inspire hope.

Emma encouraged people to join her in exploring their artistic paths by organizing seminars and group projects. By using art to find solace and meaning, she provided venues where individuals could express their stories, anxieties, and dreams. The studio became a haven for group creativity, where people could find motivation, encouragement, and bravery to follow their passions.

Emma's artwork developed as she worked on it, expressing her search for meaning and optimism. Her paintings evolved into visual narratives that told tales of tenacity, love, and the beauty that results from accepting one's true self. The neighborhood reacted warmly, taking comfort and inspiration from Emma's artistic efforts.

Emma's adventure, however, continued. She was aware of the influence her work may have on people's lives both within and outside the four walls of her studio. She coordinated international artist partnerships and shows with the help of the local community. Her art had a transformational force that extended to new horizons, inspiring people from all backgrounds and cultures with purpose, perseverance, and optimism.

Emma concluded that her search for hope and meaning had never been about arriving at a specific place as she stood before her collection of paintings and thought back on her trip. It was all about the voyage—the discovery, development, and relationships made along the way. She knew that the absolute satisfaction came from her art's effect on people's lives, not praise or recognition.

Alice's legacy sparked Emma's journey of self-discovery and artistic exploration. Still, Emma's tenacity, vulnerability, and steadfast faith in the transformative power of art enabled her to uncover her sense of hope and purpose. And in doing so, she had developed into a source of inspiration, carrying on Alice's torch while also making her stamp on the world, one brushstroke at a time.

Chapter 2

Decrypting the Past

Emma's experience in the art studio had been transforming. The renovated area has developed into a center for inspiration and innovation, resonating with tales of both Emma and Alice Turner. However, the untold stories of Alice's life that remained buried in the dark corners of the abandoned studio remained a persistent enigma that Emma could not get rid of.

Emma started investigating the past because she was curious and connected to Alice's artwork. She dug deeper into the studio's records, looking for hints that may reveal more about the mysterious artist who had once resided here. Alice's personal past was pieced together as she dug through dusty boxes and faded pictures.

Emma discovered a bundle of ancient, faded letters among the antiquities. They were conversations between Alice and her closest confidante, a cherished friend who had traveled the same path as Alice as an artist. The letters provided personal information about their goals, problems, and daily lives, providing a realistic portrait of their everyday experiences as artists.

Emma spent a lot of time reading the letters, and as she did, she discovered a story of love, sorrow, and the tenacious pursuit of artistic expression. Alice had to overcome Heartbreak, self-doubt, and the persistent worry that she would lose her creative spark. She persisted, finding comfort and motivation inside the studio's walls.

One letter, though, stuck out because it had never been mailed. It was a sincere declaration of Alice's deepest ambitions that she had written in utter vulnerability and unadulterated emotion. In the letter, Alice outlined her desire to share her talent with the world, make a difference in people's lives, and inspire optimism in others.

Emma had a strong emotional connection to Alice's unmet expectations. Alice's unsaid remarks connected with her desire for her art to have an impact. After being moved by the message, Emma decided to commemorate Alice's legacy by sharing her artwork with the world.

Emma put together a significant show honoring Alice Turner and her artistic vision with the help of the neighborhood. Along with Alice's already finished pieces, the exhibition also featured Emma's creations influenced by Alice's aesthetic and spirit. The paintings perfectly encapsulated the idea of optimism, fortitude, and the beauty that can manifest itself even in the most hopeless circumstances.

The exhibition met with great success. People of all social classes rushed to see Alice's artwork and understand its enormous effect on their lives. Emma noticed Alice's presence among the others as she stood there as if the artist's spirit mingled with the whispers of astonishment and adoration.

But the exhibition had a more astounding result: it encouraged artistic expression around the town. The tales of Alice and Emma inspired many who had never thought of themselves as artists to start exploring their creative sides. Murals and sculptures appeared all over the town, turning it into a canvas that reflected the community's newly discovered sense of purpose and hope.

After the show, Emma understood that her journey had completed a circle. Emma had found her own artistic voice and inspired others through her investigation of the abandoned studio, the discovery of Alice's letters, and the display of Alice's artwork.

The abandoned and decaying art studio has evolved into a source of inspiration and optimism, demonstrating the tenacity of artists and the strength of their works. Emma and the neighborhood that supported her revived Alice's legacy and continued it.

Emma realized as she surveyed the altered art studio that her efforts to delve into the past uncovered an intriguing tale and influenced her present and future. She had learned from the journey that art can transcend time, mend wounds, and shed light on even the most shadowy aspects of the human experience.

Thus, Emma carried on making art, incorporating Alice's legacy and her artistic path into her work by drawing inspiration from historical accounts. She expressed her gratitude to the mysterious artist who had opened the way for her creative awakening with every brushstroke, a testament to the enduring power of art and the significant impact it can have on the world.

Emma Reads Alice's Journal In Further Detail.

Emma read further into Alice's journal and found many experiences that influenced the artist's life, including emotions, challenges, and victories. The tattered pages included Alice's most private ideas, sketches, and comments, offering a window into the depths of her creative journey.

Emma's comprehension of the fundamental importance of hope in Alice's life grew as she read more. A demanding culture that frequently neglected female artists, personal traumas, and self-doubt that threatened to stifle her creative spirit were just a few of Alice's difficulties. But throughout it all, optimism had remained her compass, a pillar of fortitude that sustained her creativity.

In her notebook, Alice documented her unshakable commitment to artistic quality and her faith in the transformational power of art. Alice had found peace within the walls of the run-down workshop, pouring her heart and soul onto paintings that brought her most intense feelings to life. She had learned to manage the harsh seas of life through her art, finding beauty in even the most unremarkable circumstances.

Alice's unwavering commitment moved Emma, and became engrossed in the tales told in the journal's pages. She could feel the unadulterated vulnerability Alice had put into her work, an exposure that profoundly impacted Emma's artistic development. It was as though Alice's challenges and victories had merged with her own, tying them together across time and space.

Emma started to see Alice as a mentor, helping her discover her creative potential as an artist. She scrutinized Alice's drawings, admired her use of color, and soaked up the knowledge contained in her words. Emma learned about the significant effects that art might have on the artist's mind and the environment through Alice's journal. Emma also learned about the technical components of art.

In one particularly moving entry, Alice described a time of extreme despair when her spring of inspiration had dried up, and hope seemed like a distant memory. Emma could identify with this feeling because she had also gone through periods of creative block and insecurity. But Alice's tale reminded her that while hope could run out, it could also be grown and maintained.

Emma immersed herself in the surroundings of the studio, determined to rekindle her artistic flame. She saw the dance of light and shadow, the brilliant hues of nature, and the often-overlooked little marvels. She started to utilize her art as a way to inspire herself as well as people who saw her creations. She began to imbue her paintings with a newfound sense of hope.

Emma was deeply connected to Alice as she painted, as though they were working together on a collaborative piece of art apart in time. Emma was determined to shake the chains of self-doubt and embrace the limitless possibilities that art offered, and she found inspiration in Alice's difficulties and victories.

The neighborhood became aware of Emma's artistic path and her relationship with Alice. People rushed to the studio in droves, curious to see Emma's artwork develop and learn more about the hopeful tales she incorporated into her works. The studio evolved into a haven where people could find comfort, motivation, and new faith in their artistic undertakings.

However, Emma's examination of Alice's notebook had a second unanticipated result: it strengthened her ties to the neighborhood. She became aware that art can profoundly unify people as she told Alice's tale and the lessons she had discovered on her journey. The studio developed into a hub of creation where creators from all walks of life gathered to exchange experiences, provide support, and light a spark of hope in one another.

They collaborated on initiatives, workshops, and exhibitions that emphasized the variety of artistic expression. The studio's walls appeared as a tapestry of tales, expressing the community's tenacity, bravery, and optimism.

Emma's artistic expression kept developing, reflecting Alice's legacy's significant influence on her life. Intricacies of human emotion, the beauty of ordinary situations, and the resounding message that hope might be found even in the most challenging circumstances were all represented in her paintings. Each brushstroke contained a small expression of thanks to Alice, the teacher who had unintentionally assisted her on the path to her artistic awakening.

Emma's purpose was to inspire people, spread hope, and serve as a reminder of the transformational power of creativity. She had discovered her purpose through her work. She understood that her experience with Alice's journal had evolved into a mission to carry on Alice's legacy and inspire hope in everyone who could experience it.

Emma was overcome with gratitude as she stood before the renovated art studio. She was grateful for the chance to read through Alice's journal, the healing potential of art, and the community's support of her and her journey. She persisted in painting, sharing her tales, and making a place where hope might blossom as time passed—a lasting testimony to Alice's legacy's enormous influence on both her artistic development and the lives of others around her.

Emma Goes To The Neighborhood Library.

Emma visited the neighborhood library to learn more about how Alice's artwork affected the neighborhood. She set out to find those who had known Alice or had been affected by her artwork, armed with her notebook and genuine interest. She hoped that through hearing their experiences, people would better appreciate the significant impact Alice had on everyone around her.

Mrs. Thompson, an older woman who had lived next door to Alice for a long time, was the subject of her first interview. Warm greetings were extended to Emma, and as they sat down, Mrs.

Thompson's eyes began to light up with recollections of her cherished companion.

Mrs. Thompson recalled when Alice let neighbors and bystanders into her studio to share her paintings and have frank discussions about life and art. She talked about Alice's talent for capturing the core of the human spirit in paint and evoking feelings that language alone could not express.

Mrs. Thompson said, "People would come into the studio feeling burdened by their troubles." She had a way of putting warmth, empathy, and a hint of magic into her paintings, such that anyone who interacted with her and saw her work would leave with a refreshed sense of optimism and a lighter heart.

Emma paid close attention as the accounts of how Alice's artwork had impacted people's lives captured her attention. It was evident that Alice's writing had been a solace for the soul and an oasis of optimism in a frequently uncertain environment.

Emma resumed her interviews after hearing Mrs. Thompson's story and sought out other people who had come into contact with Alice and her artwork. She met Mr. Johnson, a local educator who told her tales of his students finding inspiration in Alice's paintings. He described how he would frequently take his class to the studio to get lost in the vivid hues and fantastic settings that Alice painted.

"The impact was profound," said Mr. Johnson. "The students would return to the classroom with a newfound passion for art, expressing themselves fearlessly and embracing their creativity. Alice's art had the power to unlock their potential, showing them that they too had the ability to create beauty in their own lives."

Emma's conversations with community members revealed numerous tales of how Alice's art had touched hearts and changed lives. She spoke with a young lady named Lily, who described how Alice's paintings had given her peace and reminded her of the resiliency of the human spirit as she struggled through a trying time of grief.

I used to sit in the workshop for hours just admiring Alice's creations, Lily recalled. "It was like her paintings whispered to me, reminding me that even amid sorrow, there is beauty to be found. Alice's art became my refuge, a source of comfort that allowed me to heal and embrace life again."

Emma's interactions with the locals clearly show Alice's ongoing effects. Her work had evolved into a mirror that reflected the aspirations, sentiments, and feelings of individuals who saw it. A sanctuary—a place where people could find comfort, inspiration, and a sense of purpose again—had been created by Alice in addition to her paintings.

With these tales at her disposal, Emma was more motivated than ever to continue Alice's legacy. In addition to Alice's artwork, she also displayed the stories she had gathered from the neighborhood at an exhibition she arranged at the studio. The display evolved into a celebration of the creative spirit of people and the unifying and uplifting abilities of art.

People from all walks of life rushed to the exhibition in droves, eager to enter Alice's universe and see her artwork's significant influence on the neighborhood. Emma heard laughter filling the air as they walked around the gallery, saw tears welling up in their eyes, and had a real sense of connection.

The show had developed into a testimony to the transformational power of art and Alice's enduring legacy of optimism. It served as a reminder that art can transcend space and time, unite disparate generations, and reach into the very core of the human soul.

Emma noticed her journey had completed a circle as she stood among the crowd. A bright tapestry of hope and inspiration had resulted from examining Alice's journal, renovating the art studio, and gathering community stories.

Emma realized at that point that she had taken on the role of Alice's art protector, acting as a conduit for the legacy of beauty and optimism to live on. She promised to uplift others through her artistic endeavors in remembrance of Alice, just as Alice had done before her.

Every time Emma would paint, she would do so with the spirit of Alice—a heart steeped in fortitude, empathy, and a firm conviction in the transforming potential of art. She would keep looking for tales, listening to those around her, and creating an environment where hope could flourish.

Emma finally understood that art is more than simply a means of self-expression; it is a gift to be shared, a lighthouse of hope to lead people through the maze of life. A brilliant tapestry of hope would be woven over the neighborhood and beyond as long as Alice kept creating and inspiring.

Finding A Hidden Painting

Emma had spent numerous hours at the former art studio poring over Alice's journal, learning about her creative process, and observing her work's enormous effects on the neighborhood. However, on that fateful day, Emma was sorting through some supplies in a forgotten studio area when she accidentally came across a hidden painting. This secret gem would drastically alter the trajectory of her artistic development.

Emma had never seen a painting like that before. It gave off a magnetic atmosphere that drew her in with an enticing intensity. Excitement rushed through her as she extended her hand to touch the canvas. It was as though the picture concealed a mystery just waiting to be discovered.

Emma reached for a neighboring easel with shaky hands and carefully placed the hidden painting there. She took a step back, and she let out a gasp. An incomplete masterpiece, the painting offered a look into a colorful and alluring universe that appeared to exist outside everyday reality.

The colors on the painting seemed to have a life of their own as they swung and danced. A tapestry of colors made up of vivid hues of scarlet, emerald, and gold interlaced with one another inspired astonishment and wonder. Even though the brushstrokes were solid and deliberate, the picture was still unfinished—it was a moment in time that was waiting for the artist's finishing touch.

The picture's underlying mystery enthralled Emma. There were traces of Alice's artistic vision left on the canvas as if she had put her entire soul upon it. She pondered the reasons behind Alice's unfinished masterwork and what it would reveal if it came to life.

Emma committed herself to solving the hidden picture's mystery because of her curiosity. She carefully read Alice's journal, looking for hints to explain its meaning. As she turned the pages, she came upon a passage that mentioned the incomplete masterpiece, a reminder of Alice's difficulties with insecurities and the never-ending search for excellence.

In the entry, Alice shared her trepidation about finishing the painting because she feared it wouldn't meet her standards. She expressed her feelings of tremendous pressure, the weight of her artistic heritage, and the terrible doubt that she could ever represent the vivid world in her head.

Emma made a solemn pledge after being moved by Alice's vulnerability. For Alice and for herself, she would finish the incomplete masterpiece. She would assume Alice's position as the artist, allowing her creative soul to converge with Alice's to achieve a long-forgotten vision.

Emma got to work with a newfound feeling of purpose. She scrutinized the brushstrokes, color blending, and minute details Alice had left behind. She lost herself in the world of the painting, letting her creativity take control, and her imagination run wild.

Days passed into weeks as Emma devoted herself entirely to finishing the masterpiece. She became absorbed in the need to bring the painting to life, losing sight of time altogether. And she experienced a strong bond with Alice with each brushstroke—a bond that was independent of time and place.

Emma backed up as the last brushstroke was applied to the canvas, gasping for air. A work-in-progress that was once buried had been converted into a bright and alluring universe, demonstrating the strength of tenacity, self-belief, and the pursuit of one's creative vision.

As soon as the finished artwork became known to the neighborhood, people hurried to the art studio to see the transformation for themselves. Their hearts grew heavy with feelings they couldn't quite express as they stared at the artwork with widening eyes of astonishment.

The picture represented optimism and served as a reminder that beauty may still be found despite doubt and uncertainty. It encouraged people to embrace their creative spirits and pursue their passions with unshakable tenacity. It talked about the goals and aspirations that lie dormant within each person.

Emma's completion of the masterpiece paid tribute to Alice's artistic heritage and rekindled the community's inspiration. The studio developed into a center for artistic inquiry where individuals from all walks of life could assemble to celebrate the transformational power of art and feed their creative spirits.

And Emma realized that her journey had been much more than just finding an unfinished work of art as she stood in the middle of the busy painting studio. It had been a journey of self-discovery, establishing her artistic voice and discovering her untapped potential.

Emma's progress as a person and artist had been sparked by the hidden painting, which also ignited a fire within her that burned brighter than ever. She painted each new creation with her distinctive style and the spirit of Alice—a continual reminder of the immense influence that art can have on the world.

The narrative of Emma, Alice, and the hidden painting eventually came together. As a result, she was serving as a testament to the ability of art to transcend space and time, unite people, and arouse hope. The studio, which had formerly been abandoned and in disrepair, now exuded a spirit of hope and innovation.

Emma couldn't help but smile as she took in the finished product. It served as a reminder that every artist's path has a hidden gem, a work of art waiting to be revealed, and a world just waiting to be explored.

The Ability Of Art To Arouse Hope.

Emma was drawn to understand more about Alice's personal life as she dug deeper into the artist's world and her work. She ached for a deeper comprehension of the person whose legacy had impacted so many people. Rose, a kind, older woman who had formerly been close to Alice, crossed Emma's path as she was doing this search.

At a nearby gallery where Alice's artworks were on show, Emma first ran into Rose. Rose sat before one of the vivid paintings, her eyes sparkling with recollections. Emma approached Rose and started a chat with her after learning about her relationship with Alice.

The two women immediately became deeply involved in a conversation about how much they admired Alice's artwork. Emma politely asked Rose if she would be prepared to share her recollections of Alice because she could tell that her aged eyes held a treasure of untold tales.

Rose's expression softened, and she smiled sentimentally. She agreed to meet Emma at the adjacent coffee shop, where they found a quiet spot and started their voyage through memories.

Rose told them a story about friendship and shared artistic aspirations while they sipped their warm tea. She recalled the times when she and Alice used to work together for hours in the studio, painting imaginative and colorful worlds on canvas with their brushes.

Rose spoke with a tint of melancholy, "Emma, you see, Alice had a steadfast belief in the power of art to inspire optimism. She believed every brushstroke could touch someone's spirit and create joy, even in the most trying circumstances.

Emma listened carefully, her heart fluttering with a fresh admiration for Alice's talent and steadfast commitment to her profession. Rose went on to describe Alice's fortitude and her capacity to see the beauty in the most essential things.

"She would often say, 'Art is a language that transcends barriers, that speaks directly to the heart,'" Rose said. "Alice saw the world through a different lens—an artist's lens—and she woven stories of hope, of resiliency, and of the inherent beauty that resides in every human being in her paintings."

Emma discovered that she was clinging to every word, mesmerized by the depth of Alice's convictions. She understood that Alice's artwork was about more than just producing aesthetically beautiful images; it was about connecting deeply with those who saw it.

Emma learned that Alice had a significant influence on the community that went beyond her work as Rose continued to relate her experiences. Inviting people from all areas of life to join together and discover their creative potential, she frequently organized painting workshops.

With a glint in her eye, Rose remarked that "people would flock to the workshops." Alice encouraged others to let go of their inhibitions, embrace their individual artistic voice, and use art as a vehicle for self-expression and healing.

Emma couldn't help but compare Alice's outlook to her own artistic development. She was inspired by the accounts of perseverance, connection, and optimism, and they strengthened her resolve to uphold Alice's legacy.

Emma and Rose developed a strong bond that cut across generational boundaries over time. Rose turned out to be Emma's guiding light, giving her insights into Alice's creative process, stories about their experiences together, and looking at the person who painted the pictures.

Rose helped Emma find more hidden treasures in Alice's studio, including a collection of sketches, unfinished paintings, and private notes that provided insight into Alice's creative process. Emma combed through these artifacts, immersing herself in Alice's creative process and finding motivation in each brushstroke.

Emma began to see the significant impact she could have on her community due to her contacts with Rose and her investigation of Alice's artwork. She recognized the ability of art to close gaps, mend hurts, and inspire a sense of possibility.

Emma set up her own art workshops, just as Alice had done years earlier, with a newfound sense of purpose. Children, teenagers, adults, and seniors from all walks of life were asked to come together and learn about the transformational power of art. She pushed students to embrace their creativity, let go of self-doubt, and trust in the beauty that already lives inside them.

The workshops evolved into a place of openness, community, and development. Participants expressed themselves through the language of art, sharing their experiences, hopes, and dreams. Emma realized she was continuing Alice's legacy of inspiration and optimism as she saw the positive impact art had on the lives of those around her.

Emma and Rose became role models for inventiveness and resiliency in their neighborhood. They worked together to organize art exhibits featuring regional artists' works and communicated a message of harmony and hope. The abandoned and decaying art studio was transformed into a thriving center for artistic expression where people could find comfort, support, and a sense of community.

Emma couldn't help but feel profound appreciation for the unexpected meeting with Rose as she sat among the vibrant energy of the art studio, surrounded by Alice's paintings and the creations of aspiring artists. Emma had discovered the spirit of Alice's artwork through Rose's stories and advice, but she had also found her own artistic voice—a voice that held Alice's unshakeable faith in the ability of art to inspire hope.

And as Emma and Rose hugged each other, they were filled with pride in the knowledge that Alice's legacy would continue to touch the lives of countless people, inspire hope, and create a tapestry of beauty within their community and beyond, thanks to their shared love of art.

An Unfinished Painting Interpreted

Emma set off on a quest to finish the unfinished masterpiece she had uncovered in the art studio—the painting that had caught her imagination and touched her soul—with a renewed feeling of purpose and inspiration. Emma set out to construct her own vision of the colorful and alluring world portrayed in the hidden picture, guided by Alice's legacy and the tales she had learned from Rose and the locals.

Emma inhaled as she assumed a position before the white canvas, her heart racing with anticipation. The rich hues on her palette—crimson, blue, and gold—represented the emotions that flowed through her when she dipped her brush into them. She infused the painting with her distinctive voice by pouring her experiences, dreams, and hopes onto the canvas with each stroke.

The way the colors moved and entwined reflected Emma's intensity of feeling. She painted with a passion she had never felt, motivated by the conviction that art could uplift and inspire. The brush captured her sentiments on canvas as it glided across the surface with ease.

Emma experienced a strong bond with Alice as the picture started to take shape—a bond that transcended time and geography. She interpreted Alice's artistic vision and infused it with her understanding of herself in her brushstrokes, capturing the essence of it. The painting turned into a reflection of her soul, showing her journey and the change she had undergone.

As Emma put her heart and soul into the painting, days became weeks and weeks into months. She painted quickly to spread her newfound inspiration and sense of hope to everyone. The studio became her haven, a place where she could lose herself in the abyss of her imagination and come out with a work of art that could stir the soul and light a fire of hope.

Emma stepped back as the final stroke of the brush touched the canvas, tears welling in her eyes. The artwork in front of her symbolized her development, tenacity, and everlasting faith in the transformative power of art. It was evidence of her life-changing trip, following in Alice's footsteps and touching the hearts of everyone who saw her work.

When Emma's artwork was finished, word quickly went around the neighborhood. The vivid colors and the raw passion that radiated from the painting drew visitors from far and wide to the art studio. They felt the rush of inspiration and hope emanating from Emma's creation as they stood before it; their breath stopped in their throats.

As a visual reflection of each person's strength and beauty, Emma's painting grew to become a beacon of light. It discussed how the human spirit can overcome obstacles, accept weakness, and find strength in pursuing ambitions. Emma had made a place where people could connect, exchange stories, and find hope even in the most challenging circumstances through her work.

However, many were impacted by the painting in more ways than one. How Emma listened, shared, and appreciated other people's stories helped create a human connection through her job. People found comfort, acceptance, and a sense of belonging in the art studio, which evolved into a space for healing.

Emma had learned from her experience that art was more than just producing beautiful things. The goal was to create an environment where people could feel heard, seen, and understood. It was about evoking feelings and starting conversations using colors, shapes, and textures.

It was about using art to express ideas of resilience, hope, and the boundless potential that each and every person possesses.

Emma became aware that her journey had gone beyond the confines of herself as she stood in the middle of the busy art studio, surrounded by other people's crafts and the lively spirit of the neighborhood. She had evolved into a force for change, an inspiration to people who had lost their way or forgotten the strength of their aspirations.

Thus, Emma's adventure carried on as she was entwined with the tales of Alice, Rose, and the several people she had met along the way. Her paintings praised the human spirit, sparked change, and spoke directly to the hearts of those who saw them. She began painting with a newfound feeling of purpose.

Emma's artwork attained more acclaim in the following years. Her artwork was displayed in galleries and museums, crossing national boundaries and cultural barriers to represent the unifying language of optimism and grit. She used her position to make other people's voices heard, bring attention to social issues, and promote communication and understanding.

Emma remained a grounded artist who recognized the underlying impact of her work, even in the face of praise and acclaim. She continued going to the neighborhood library, hearing the older woman's tales, and mentoring young artists developing their unique artistic voices.

Like Alice, Emma left a lasting legacy far beyond her artistic endeavors. It left behind a legacy of human connection, encouraging people to explore their own creativity and serving as a constant reminder to the globe that despite chaos and uncertainty, there is always a glimmer of hope waiting to be revealed.

And Emma took the tales, the lessons, and the steadfast faith in the transformational power of art within her as she stood before a fresh blank canvas, prepared to begin her next artistic adventure. She understood that she could change things, one brushstroke at a time, just as Alice had made her mark on the world.

Chapter 3

The Path of Hope

She had always had a strong passion for painting, but recently a dark cloud of despair had descended upon her. Her palette's colors had become lifeless, and her once-vibrant brushstrokes appeared dead.

One day, as Emma strolled through her town's cobblestone streets, she found an old bookshop tucked away in a corner. She chose to enter after being intrigued by its beaten-up exterior. As she browsed the racks, her fingertips delicately stroking the spines of the long-forgotten tales, the musty aroma of old books permeated the room.

A book titled "The Journey of Hope" caught Emma's attention as she was lost in thought; the cover showed a winding route lined with colorful flowers that stretched to the horizon. She became intrigued by the story waiting to be revealed within its pages due to her curiosity.

She found a comfortable spot in the bookstore and let the book carry her to a world where optimism blossomed even in dire circumstances. Young Lily, the main character, set out on a mission to locate a legendary place where hope ruled supreme. Lily's adventure led her through difficult woods, choppy seas, and into the hearts of the individuals she met.

As Emma became engrossed in Lily's tale, she saw that hope was more than just an idealized idea; it was a natural force that could alter people's lives. It served as a guiding light for lost souls, repaired broken hearts, and rekindled the inspiration of the worn-out.

Lily's exploits gave Emma the desire to set out on her hopeful quest. She yearned for a means to escape the chains of hopelessness that had imprisoned her creative spirit. She had no idea optimism would eventually find her in the most unlikely places.

Emma came across an outdated, derelict art studio one bright afternoon while exploring the town's outskirts. Its ancient walls served as a reminder of the passage of time, and an eerie air surrounded the building. Curious, she pulled open the squeaky door and entered the lost world.

The aroma of dried paint and memories permeated the interior. Dust-covered paintings whispered tales of their genesis. The tattered journal was tucked away in a corner and caught Emma's attention as she inspected the space. It belonged to a forgotten artist named Alice Turner, who had once lived in this studio.

Opening the diary with shaky hands, Emma found pages full of lovely doodles, poetic reflections, and insights into Alice's inner world. She learned about Alice's challenges, victories, and the significant influence her painting had on the neighborhood during trying times. Emma's optimism started reviving as she learned more about Alice's tale.

Emma searched to get in touch with Alice's acquaintances to learn more about the artist's legacy. She went to the neighborhood library to find people who could provide insight into Alice's life and the significance of her work. People reminisced about the happiness, serenity, and inspiration they had experienced while viewing Alice's artwork at the library, which evolved into a haven of shared tales.

Emma once encountered an older woman named Rose while browsing the library's shelves. Emma sensed an unexplainable connection when they shared a moment of recognition. Rose had been Alice's close friend, with whom she had gone on innumerable creative trips and had deep chats.

Emma found a wealth of insight and memories when she spent time with Rose. Rose mentioned Alice's unshakeable faith in the capacity of art to uplift the human spirit—a belief passed down through artists' generations. Emma understood via Rose's experiences that the journey of hope was a single attempt and a group effort woven through the threads of interpersonal connection.

Emma returned to the art studio, her veins bursting with fresh inspiration. She found a hidden painting—an incomplete masterpiece—among the abandoned canvases and dirty easels. Emma was drawn to bring the colors on the canvas to life because they seemed to vibrate with the possibility of something remarkable.

Emma pulled up her paintbrushes and started painting, motivated by her burgeoning hope and Alice's legacy. She painted fervently, bringing vivid colors to the canvas and communicating her feeling of purpose. As the painting neared completion, Emma experienced a great sense of fulfillment. Each brushstroke rang with whispers of optimism.

After the painter had finished, Emma stood back and gazed in awe at the finished piece. It painted a picture of a colorful world where opportunities were endless, and ambitions could fly. It served as a visual symbol of Emma's journey and the resiliency of the human spirit, and it was a monument to the transformational power of hope.

Town residents began flocking to the art studio like moths to a flame as word of Emma's painting spread throughout the community. They felt the jolt of inspiration and optimism emanating from the painting as they stood before it, their eyes ablaze with wonder. They found their glimmer of hope and the conviction that they could set off on their transformational journeys amid Emma's work.

As a result, Emma's painting began to represent hope within the neighborhood and served as a focal point for those who were dreamers, creators, and searchers of inspiration. It provided a timely reminder that the depths of artistic expression and the strength of human connection might be sources of hope even in the most hopeless circumstances.

Emma realized that her journey of hope had only just begun as she regarded the painting and basked in the glow of its influence. She realized that pursuing hope was a lifelong endeavor—a flame that needed to be maintained and spread— rather than an end. And Emma would keep igniting the flame of hope within herself and others, giving brilliant colors to a world that yearned for their brilliance, with each brushstroke, each connection forged, and each narrative recounted.

The Understanding

The impact of Emma's remarkable artwork was felt far and wide as word of it went throughout the neighborhood. The brilliant colors and seeming sense of hope emanating from the canvas drew visitors from all walks of life to the art studio. Emma's artwork evolved into a source of hope, comfort in difficult times, and a reminder of the strength of fortitude and hope.

An article on Emma's travels and her work's significant impact on the neighborhood was published in the neighborhood newspaper. The tale moved readers, and Emma soon began receiving requests to display her work at museums and art fairs. Her works, each a tribute to the magnificence and fortitude of the human spirit, started to adorn the walls of esteemed art organizations.

Emma, however, did not let praise and recognition motivate her to create. She didn't waver, humbled by her art's effect on other people. She knew her artwork spoke to people's hearts in a language other than merely the vibrant brushstrokes on the canvas. She valued the power to make a difference in people's lives, start conversations, and effect change above all else.

Despite her increasing fame, Emma stayed committed to her neighborhood. She planned painting classes for kids, urging them to use color and shape to express their emotions. She spoke at nearby schools, inspiring children to follow their creative passions without fear by sharing her narrative of hope and resiliency.

Emma was allowed to speak at a community event one day when people who had experienced hardship and sought comfort and motivation were gathered. She addressed the audience while standing there, sharing her own story of desperation, discovery, and the transforming power of art. Her comments struck a deep chord with the crowd, bringing tears to their eyes and sparking hope in their hearts.

There was a little pause when Emma finished speaking, as though everyone in the room was holding their breath. The tremendous symphony of admiration and thankfulness then broke out in the form of applause. Individuals approached

Emma individually and related their experiences with how her work had impacted them. Others expressed how the colors and shapes she produced had brought them peace. Some talked of having the strength to follow their aspirations. Every encounter strengthened Emma's faith in the durability of the human spirit and the universality of hope.

Emma's eyes caught the attention of a little girl in the crowd, whose face was engraved with a combination of fragility and tenacity. Her name was Mia, and like many other people, she had struggled. Mia cautiously approached Emma while holding a little sketchbook close to her heart.

Mia said in a shaky voice, "I've always loved art. However, somewhere along the line, I lost hope. Your paintings remind me that there is still hope for me.

Emma snatched the sketchbook away from Mia as her heart filled with compassion. She carefully turned the pages, exposing beautiful sketches brimming with unfiltered passion and untapped promise.

Emma responded with sincerity in her voice, "Mia, your painting is lovely. "Don't let go of that spark of hope; you have a gift, and I believe there is a world of untapped possibilities within you."

Mia nodded with tears in her eyes as she did so, feeling inspired by Emma's words of support. In that instant, Emma realized that her work had gone beyond the canvas and started a transformation by encouraging others to believe in their inherent power and creative potential.

Since then, Emma has evolved from being merely an artist to serving as a role model and a source of inspiration for other aspiring artists in her community. Young artists were given access to her art studio to develop their skills, share ideas, and find comfort in a welcoming artistic environment.

Years went by, and Emma's influence only grew. Her artwork might be seen on the walls of galleries and museums and public places like hospitals and community centers. Each painting conveyed a narrative of overcoming hardship, discovering beauty in the most mundane things, and the perseverance of the human spirit.

Emma had a great sense of thankfulness as she sat in front of a fresh canvas with a paintbrush in her hands. She appreciated the path that had brought her to this place, the individuals who had impacted her life, and the chance to encourage others via her art.

Emma painted the painting with all of her heart and soul, filling it with the hues of optimism, grit, and the enduring strength of the human spirit. And as she took a step back to admire her work, she couldn't help but experience a wave of emotion—a fulfillment that went beyond any material success.

For Emma, the ultimate evaluation of her work was not found in the accolades it received or the museums it graced. It was evident in the lives it changed, the hearts it touched, and the hope it sparked. She had found her calling, her reason for being: to be a messenger of hope, a painter of feelings, and a chronicler of the human condition.

Then, as Emma took in her colorful creation, she realized it would be a constant reminder that despite adversity, hope always managed to light the road forward. Emma's art would serve as a testament to the strength and beauty of the human spirit.

The Color of Hope Exhibition

Emma was surrounded by her colorful paintings that brought life to the canvas as she stood in her studio. Her accomplishment as an artist gave her joy and improved the lives of many people in her neighborhood. She was incredibly grateful and wanted to return the favor by building a foundation on which optimism could thrive despite her brushstrokes.

Emma's mind began to race as she studied her creation. She decided to plan an art exhibition called "The Color of Hope," which would honor art's fortitude and transforming potential. Her paintings would be on display, but the exhibition would also include hopeful testimonies from people in her neighborhood. It would serve as a celebration of the human spirit and a reminder that even in the most hopeless circumstances, there is always reason for optimism.

Emma set out to bring her vision to life with excitement coursing through her blood. She invited individuals to contribute their inspirational experiences by contacting neighborhood community centers, schools, and organizations. To evoke emotion in visitors and encourage them to embrace optimism in their own lives, she set out to weave together a diverse tapestry of experiences and a collection of anecdotes.

The response was tremendous. People from all walks of life approached, eager to share their experiences of overcoming hardship, discovering hope in the face of despair, and the incredible strength of human perseverance. Emma listened closely to each tale, her heart swelling with admiration and sympathy for those who had overcome their obstacles to become stronger.

She meticulously woven the participants' stories into the exhibition's framework by spending endless hours with them. Written narratives would be used to tell some stories, while collaborative artworks, multimedia installations, and sculptures would be used to express others. Emma thought that art might go beyond words and help people experience and comprehend emotions more intensely.

The art studio was excited as the exhibition's opening day drew near. Emma and her group put in a lot of effort to turn the area into a gallery that would inspire amazement and introspection. Her colorful paintings, each of which was accompanied by a moving account of hope, decorated the walls. The studio was filled with a contagious spirit that was infused with expectation.

The community gathered to see the realization of Emma's vision on "The Color of Hope" opening night. Visitors mingled with artists and storytellers, sharing their stories and forging connections through a common appreciation of the human spirit. The room was buzzing with excitement.

Emma stepped back as the show was formally opened, her gaze scanning the space. Visitors looked at the artwork intently, their expressions varying from amazement to reflection to tears of resonance. The stories' profundity and honesty affected the audience, and Emma felt a range of feelings, including joy, humility, and a deep appreciation.

Visitors were encouraged to interact with the artwork and tales throughout the show, think about their journeys, and take comfort in the hope that emanated from the walls. The gallery evolved into a place of solace and kinship where strangers found common ground, exposed their frailties, and supported one another.

Inside the gallery, Emma saw instances of profound human connection. A couple holding hands found comfort in the image that captured their shared adversity and the hope that had carried them through. The tales moved a young painter, and, after a long absence, picked up a brush again, rekindling her love and relocating her source of hope.

The effects of the exhibition extended well beyond the confines of the art studio. As word of "The Color of Hope's" transformational impact traveled through the media, the artists' and storytellers' accounts resonated with people all around the area. Visitors from nearby towns and cities flocked to the show, captivated by the appeal of art woven with threads of optimism.

Emma received letters and comments from people affected by the exhibition in the following weeks. They related tales of how the art pieces had rekindled their faith in the human spirit's capacity, how the stories had given them the courage to face their difficulties, and how hope had come to serve as a beacon in their life.

Emma understood that her work had been transformed into a symbol of the community's aspirations and aspirations, serving as a concrete reminder that there was always hope to be had. She realized that her role as an artist involved more than just producing stunning works; it also involved developing relationships, igniting social change, and reminding people of their inherent power.

Long after the exhibition closed, "The Color of Hope" changed people's lives. To reach a larger audience, Emma and her team partnered with community centers and schools to present the artwork and stories. The exhibition went on the road as a showcase, inspiring people to embrace their creative paths and sharing its message of optimism and resiliency with various communities.

Emma couldn't help but feel overwhelmed by a sense of fulfillment as she considered "The Color of Hope's" influence. She had created a space via art where people could express their feelings, hear triumphant and resilient tales, and celebrate optimism as a potent force for change.

In the end, Emma's journey had been one of connection, personal development, and artistic discovery, demonstrating the significant influence one person's optimism and creativity could have on a community. Emma realized that the journey of hope will always be bound up with the strength of human emotion and the enduring tenacity of the human spirit as she went on to paint, tell tales, and inspire others via her work.

Difficulties And Self-Doubt

Emma encountered unforeseen difficulties while preparing for the "The Color of Hope" show and struggled with occasional self-doubt. She felt the pressure of responsibility since she was aware of the significant influence her art may have on other people. She began to wonder whether her effort was worthwhile and whether she could inspire optimism through her paintings.

As Emma labored in her art studio, searching for the ideal brushstrokes and color combinations to express the essence of optimism, the days turned into nights. But the more she made an effort to force inspiration, the harder it was to find. She began to feel frustrated and began to doubt her artistic ability.

Emma sat among her unfinished paintings one evening, tears flowing down her face, exhausted and discouraged. She questioned her ability to live up to the standards she had set for herself and whether her work could inspire others' hope. Her soul had been infiltrated by doubt, which had dulled the festive spirit that had led her thus far.

Emma looked at a modest, unfinished artwork that was hidden in a studio corner during that precarious time. Emma's path of hope was motivated by Alice Turner's unfinished masterwork. A surge of insight washed over her as she stretched out and traced the strokes Alice had left behind.

Emma understood that uncertainty was a regular aspect of the creative process and that even the most well-known artists had experienced it. It was important not to give in to those uncertainties but to overcome them and find the fortitude to press on despite the shadows looming over her brightness.

Emma went out to re-establish a connection with her source of hope with fresh vigor. She started taking long strolls through the wilderness, letting the splendor of the environment permeate her senses. She immersed herself in art disciplines outside her own, seeking solace in the poetry and music of others.

Through this reflection, Emma realized that hope was a flame that existed within her existence rather than something external to be grabbed. She realized that her art served as a channel for that innate optimism, a means by which she could share her story of resiliency and encourage others to find their light sources.

After gaining this new insight, Emma returned to her studio with her brushes poised with purpose. She let go of the need to produce anything impressive and permitted herself to enjoy the creative process. She toyed with colors, tried various techniques, and let her feelings dictate each stroke.

Weeks passed into days, and Emma's artwork started to change due to her inward development. Every canvas conveyed a tale of resiliency, optimism, and the triumph of the human spirit. They emanated a raw realism. She accepted her flaws because she understood genuine connections were made when people were vulnerable.

Emma, however, had yet another challenge as the show date approached. The event's planning and organization seemed incredibly complex. Resurfacing doubts about her ability to handle the scope of the exhibition she had imagined arose. She was in danger of losing the spark of optimism she had rekindled because of self-doubt.

Emma sought out those who had helped her along the way in her moment of desperation. She resorted to her loved ones, close friends, and the neighborhood that had warmly welcomed her work. She could continue because of their unfailing faith in her and their guarantees.

Emma also understood that she did not have to handle the difficulties alone. She invited her other artists to work together and contribute their knowledge to the exhibition to get their support. Her spirit was revived by the sense of community and a common goal, which reminded her that she was not alone in her quest to spread optimism via art.

They banded together and put forth endless effort to plan the logistics, select the artworks, and ensure that every aspect of the exhibition was painstakingly taken care of. Together, the obstacles looked more doable to overcome, and Emma's resolve grew stronger daily.

The day of the exhibition eventually came, marking the end of Emma's journey, her victory against self-doubt, and a tribute to the strength of hope. Visitors poured in when the gallery doors opened, their eyes bright with anticipation.

Emma saw the transforming power of hope manifest in front of her eyes as she observed people immersing themselves in the artwork. The stories that were incorporated into each picture drove viewers to tears and touched their hearts. They conversed while exchanging personal tales of resiliency and hope. People who had never met could connect and become friends through the exhibition.

Emma stood in the middle of the vivid paintings, her heart overflowing with admiration and thanks. In light of her art's enormous effect on others, she no longer gave much thought to the questions that had troubled her. She understood that her exhibition's goal to create a place where hope might blossom, the human spirit could be raised, and people could find comfort and inspiration had been achieved.

A small girl approached Emma in the middle of the display, her eyes wide with astonishment. She said that doubts had prevented her from pursuing her own artistic goals. Emma knelt and revealed her struggle with self-doubt in a kind and compassionate voice.

She urged the young girl to embrace her creativity and reassured her that uncertainty was merely a stepping stone on the development path. Emma offered the young woman a paintbrush and a gentle smile, urging her to add her hopeful strokes to the group canvas in the middle of the exhibition.

Emma saw that her show had inspired hope and sparked a flame within others, encouraging them to pursue their creative journeys as the young girl's eyes gleamed with possibility. She knew that the potential to inspire hope was a shared force that could change lives and was not limited to her art.

Emma eventually realized that hope was a journey rather than a destination. She had set out on this adventure because she was passionate about art and had a firm conviction in the resiliency of the human spirit. She also realized that her work had transformed into a beacon, pointing others toward their journeys of hope, healing, and self-discovery when she saw the impact of "The Color of Hope" show.

Emma saw that she had evolved beyond being a painter to become a messenger of hope and a representative of the human spirit with each picture, each narrative, and each connection she had made. She was aware that her personal journey of hope would always be connected to the travels of people whose lives she had touched as she carried on painting, telling her experiences, and inspiring others.

Ultimately, Emma constructed an exhibition that would touch the hearts of many, thanks to her victory over self-doubt and her unwavering pursuit of optimism. And as she stood amidst the sea of colorful artwork and inspired faces, she realized that her role as an artist was to inspire hope in every person she came in contact with along the way and create beauty.

The Unmistakable Success

An aura of expectation permeated the room as "The Color of Hope" exhibition's doors swung wide. As she saw people from all walks of life fill the gallery space, Emma's pulse beat with excitement and nerves. Each person in the unique tapestry was carrying their troubles and aspirations while looking to the art waiting for them for comfort and inspiration.

Emma's vivid paintings, each a monument to the tenacity of the human spirit, were displayed on the gallery walls. The hues merged and danced, weaving tales of victory, development, and the courageous force of hope. The accompanying stories gave Each piece of art depth and meaning, which moved the hearts of those who took the time to read and comprehend them.

Emma watched from a distance as the show developed and noticed her work's profound effect on the audience. She observed the calm contemplation as they became engrossed in the story depicted in the paintings, saw tears gleaming in their eyes, and heard whispers of admiration and wonder.

Everyone who approached a specific painting, "The Phoenix's Journey," appeared mesmerized by it. It featured a magnificent phoenix emerging from the ashes with wings spread wide and aflame with vivid colors. The artwork embodied a universal symbol of rebirth and fortitude, expressing people's desire to overcome hardship and become stronger.

Emma received many letters and notes from visitors as the days and weeks after the exhibition passed. They spoke from the bottom of their hearts about how the artworks had moved them profoundly and emotionally. Strangers forged friendships after discovering comfort and inspiration in the show together.

Emma saw one letter in particular. It came from Sarah, a woman enduring a severe illness. Sarah described how the exhibition had evolved into a haven for her, where she could briefly flee the suffering and find comfort in the hues and tales revealed.

Sarah described how the artwork had renewed her hope and reminded her that beauty and power could be found even in the most challenging circumstances. She expressed her increased resolve to face her disease head-on with courage and fortitude, gaining vigor from the pieces of art that had moved her deeply.

Emma was overcome with emotion as she read Sarah's writing. Moments like these, she reinforced her faith in the ability of art to heal and inspire. She realized that her purpose involved more than just producing beautiful paintings; it also involved building relationships, starting conversations, and motivating change in people's lives.

Local media sources were interested in the exhibition because of its success. Emma was asked on television and in the press to discuss how "The Color of Hope" came to be. She used the interviews to discuss the value of resiliency, hope, and the therapeutic potential of art. The message affected Wider audiences, and soon crowds from nearby communities and even other cities gathered to visit the show.

As the exhibition's closing days drew near, Emma couldn't help but experience a bittersweet range of feelings. She had never imagined such a massive response, but she was aware that this chapter was coming to an end. She wanted to ensure the exhibition's influence would survive, yet she persisted in her dedication to fostering optimism.

Emma decided to compile the paintings, tales, and testimonies from the exhibition into a book with the assistance of her newly discovered artistic community. The novel would be an enduring example of the capacity for hope and the transformational power of art. More people would be able to hear the stories and be inspired by them, changing lives even after the show was over.

The book's writing process was both challenging and cathartic. Emma and her group gave their all to encapsulating the exhibition's spirit in its pages. To symbolize the journey of optimism and resiliency that had developed, they painstakingly picked the artworks, matched them with moving anecdotes, and carefully created the story.

When the book was ultimately released, it was well-received. It turned into a source of motivation and ended up in the hands of people looking for comfort and hope. Numerous notes from readers affected by the book, explaining how it had gotten them through their challenges and rekindled their trust in the strength of hope, were sent to Emma.

The popularity of the "The Color of Hope" exhibition and the publication of the book that followed gave Emma additional opportunities. She received offers to work with other people on various initiatives encouraging hope and healing through art, and she was invited to exhibit her work in galleries across the nation. Her journey was now intertwined with the travels of everyone she had touched, taking on a life of its own.

But despite the praise and admiration from others, Emma maintained her sense of reality. The genuine connections she had created and the difference she had made in people's lives, not the external affirmation, were how she knew she had succeeded. She carried on painting, telling tales, and inspiring people with her steadfast faith in the strength of hope.

Years later, Emma saw that her work had evolved into a vehicle for societal healing as she reflected on her path. In addition to inspiring people, the exhibition fostered a sense of belonging, a global support system, and cross-cultural empathy.

People affected by "The Color of Hope" exhibition's message continued to carry its legacy in their hearts. They incorporated the tales spoken within its walls into their narratives, which constantly inspired them to endure, see the beauty amid hardship, and maintain hope even in the most challenging circumstances.

Emma realized that her trip was far from ending as she stood in front of her easel with a brush. She vowed to keep delving into the depths of her creativity, utilize art as a catalyst for change, and spread hope wherever it was needed. Emma had learned that hope, like art, has the capacity to transform, heal, and bring people together. She would be there, prepared to paint the hues that would enlighten their journeys as long as souls yearned for hope.

Hopefulness And Creativity

Emma had transformed her artistic voyage of self-discovery. She discovered her sense of optimism and sparked a flame in the hearts of people around her as she immersed herself in creating, interacting with others, and accepting her vulnerabilities.

The influence of "The Color of Hope" exhibition and word of Emma's artistic pursuits spread like wildfire throughout the neighborhood. People from all walks of life started to take notice and were eager to witness the transformative impact of art personally. The neighborhood schools got in touch and asked Emma if she would do seminars and talk to pupils who were feeling hopeless about their situation.

Emma embraced the chance with wide arms. She thought creativity might serve as a compass, especially for the younger generation, who frequently confronted several difficulties and insecurities. She discussed her experience with self-doubt and how art had become her haven, her way of expressing herself and finding hope even in the most challenging circumstances.

Emma saw each child's fantastic potential while participating in the sessions. She urged students to trust in the transforming potential of their artistic activities and embrace their creativity and unique ideas. As they painted, the kids' faces lighted up with excitement, their minds going wild with views and hues.

Emma continues to interact with the neighborhood through a variety of outreach initiatives. She set up art therapy sessions for those dealing with mental health concerns, utilizing the creative process as a form of self-expression and healing. People found comfort in the companionship of others who understood their challenges during these sessions when they felt free to discuss their experiences and let their emotions flow into the canvas.

Sarah, one of the participants, revealed how the art therapy sessions had helped her overcome her years-long despair. She found a new way to express her feelings through painting, using color and brushstrokes to negotiate the complexity of her inner world. Sarah's apparent metamorphosis moved the group, and her renewed optimism motivated them to pursue their artistic endeavors.

Emma's efforts had an effect that went beyond the confines of the neighborhood. Art lovers and philanthropists worldwide heard about her tale and the success of the "The Color of Hope" show. Along with Emma's artistic ability, they were intrigued by the extent of her dedication to using art to spread hope and change people's lives.

Emma consequently got offers to exhibit her work in famous galleries and even got money to support her future artistic aspirations. The praise humbled her, but she didn't waver in her commitment to work that would move people's hearts and spur them to action.

Emma opened a community art center where people of all ages and backgrounds could assemble, create, and find refuge with newly discovered resources and assistance. The art center would act as a venue for collaborations, exhibitions, and workshops, encouraging a sense of community, creativity, and hope.

The art center's inaugural day is to celebrate optimism, grit, and the triumph of the human spirit. The walls were covered with Emma's paintings, each depicting a moment of personal development and change. Visitors poured in, eager to explore the colorful art world that awaited them, with eyes alight with excitement and expectation.

Amidst the merry talk of artists, students, and community members, Emma stood in the middle of the art gallery. She felt deeply fulfilled as she observed individuals pursuing their artistic passions and encouraging and supporting one another.

The art center quickly developed into a hive of activity where people could find inspiration, interact with others who shared their interests, and find their optimism. Emma led courses where she urged participants to express themselves creatively and openly. The art center's walls soon appeared as a tapestry of many aesthetics, viewpoints, and narratives.

The art center had a significant effect. Families found comfort in making art together, strengthening their ties, and encouraging honest conversation. Older people discovered a revitalized sense of purpose as they taught and imparted their experience to younger artists. And some who had previously felt alone or invisible found a sense of belonging inside the encouraging and welcoming group that had emerged.

One day, a girl named Lily approached Emma as she was strolling through the busy art center. Domestic violence victim Lily struggled with feelings of fear and helplessness. She mustered the fortitude to look for solace inside the art center's confines after learning about it and the transforming potential of art.

Lily told Emma her tale while tears were running down her face. She described how creating art had become her lifeline, a way to reclaim her voice and find courage in her weakness. Through her artwork, Lily had started to mend, to reassemble her fractured sense of self, and to rekindle a spark of hope that had been long dormant.

Emma embraced Lily as her heart swelled with sympathy and respect for the girl's fortitude. She was aware that Lily's narrative was just one of many that attested to the eternal ability of art to inspire and heal.

The art center prospered over the years, becoming a beacon of hope for the neighborhood. Emma's paintings received widespread acclaim, but her accurate fulfillment came from seeing how her clients' lives improved and developed.

Emma had come a long way from the young artist who had stumbled across the abandoned art studio. She had left a legacy that would last for many generations due to her unshakeable faith in the transformative power of art and her dedication to fostering optimism.

She couldn't help but feel a deep feeling of gratitude as she gazed at the colorful paintings that adorned the art center's walls—for the road that had brought her here, for the lives she had touched, and for the enduring beauty of human tenacity and the transformative power of hope.

Chapter 4

The Hope Legacy

Through her artistic activities and involvement in the community, Emma left behind a legacy of optimism that had deeply embedded roots in the hearts of the people she had impacted. It had evolved into a beacon, a reminder that despite life's difficulties, there was always a reason for optimism.

The legacy of hope grew as news of Emma's transforming journey and the influence of her paintings traveled beyond. People around the world got in touch with one another to share their personal accounts of how Emma's artwork and message motivated them to persist and discover their optimism in the face of hardship.

Emma received letters, emails, and messages from those who had come across her work online, at galleries, or in the pages of "The Color of Hope" book. Each letter contained a monument to the ability of art to change people's lives and the enduring effects of one person's will to inspire others.

Emma saw one message in particular. It came from a young lady named Maya, who had spent years battling a severe disease. Maya related how she had come upon one of Emma's drawings amid a very trying period in her life. She had been tremendously moved by the vivid hues and the spirit of hope that radiated from the painting, giving her the willpower to keep fighting and never lose sight of her goals.

Emma was moved by Maya's narrative, which reminded her of the significant effect that art can have on people's lives. Emma decided to start a scholarship program for young artists suffering hardship to continue her legacy of hope. The program was designed to help budding artists without the finances or opportunities to pursue their creative talents. It also offered mentorship and resources.

Talented artists from around the world submitted applications, each with distinct tales of tenacity and tenacity. Emma carefully considered each application, working with a panel of respected artists and community leaders to choose recipients whose artistic vision and individual journeys embodied the spirit of hope.

These artists found hope and opportunity in the scholarship program, which allowed them to develop their skills, go after their goals, and use art to express themselves. The legacy of hope Emma had planted grew and flourished, spreading out into the lives of these young artists who, in turn, encouraged others via their artistic pursuits.

The effects of the scholarship program and Emma's continuous dedication to fostering optimism through her work were greatly amplified. The results of scholarship recipients were displayed in galleries and public spaces as installations and exhibitions, attracting audiences with their profundity, ingenuity, and messages of resiliency.

Documentaries about Emma's life and the legacy of hope she left behind encouraged many worldwide to believe in their capacity to bring about change through creativity and steadfast hope. More than Emma could have ever anticipated, her work had a far-reaching impact that resulted in forming a global community of artists, activists, and people bound together by a shared conviction in the transformative power of art and hope.

Over time, Emma's name came to represent inspiration and hope. However, Emma focused on utilizing her art as a catalyst for change, to improve communities, and to empower people to embrace their unique journeys. Her paintings continued to be sought after by collectors and art enthusiasts.

Emma left behind a legacy of hope that was weaved into a tapestry of compassion, ingenuity, and human resiliency. It crossed barriers of space and time, leaving a lasting impression on the world and serving as a reminder to future generations that hope can be found, fostered, and shared even in the most hopeless circumstances.

And Emma couldn't help but feel more fulfilled as she considered the lives she had touched, the artists she had encouraged, and the communities she had uplifted. Hope had been the only thing holding her path together, and she had personally experienced its transformational power. She understood that her legacy would flourish and continue to provide light and inspiration to the globe for countless generations as long as art was produced, stories were told, and hope was sparked.

Collectors And Art Critics

Emma posed in front of a selection of her finished pieces of art that represented her path of self-discovery and the strength of optimism. The exhibition hall's passersby were enthralled by the paintings' vivid colors, deft brushstrokes, and evocative compositions.

Emma had no idea that her show, "The Color of Hope," would attract the interest of influential art critics and collectors in addition to art enthusiasts. The meaningful message she was able to convey through her art and her remarkable talent spread like wildfire.

Emma once got an unexpected call as she was getting ready to close the exhibition for the day. It came from Isabel Montgomery, a well-known art critic who had been to the exhibit earlier in the week. The pleasure in Isabel's voice as she described her thoughts on Emma's artwork, was palpable.

Isabel said, "Emma, your paintings have remarkably affected me. "I believe you have a great future ahead of you. Your art speaks to the depths of the human soul. Your ability to translate emotions and the essence of hope onto canvas is truly remarkable."

Emma's heart pounded with excitement. Beyond her wildest expectations, she was honored to get such compliments and recognition from someone of Isabel Montgomery's standing. Isabel continued by saying she was a writer for a prestigious art publication and intended to highlight Emma and her work in a future article.

Emma agreed to the feature out of sheer appreciation. She had no idea this piece would mark a turning point in her artistic development. The publication of Isabel's piece aroused a great deal of interest in Emma's artwork, drawing gallery owners and art collectors worldwide.

The offers to display Emma's artwork in renowned galleries began. She received requests for worldwide exhibitions and invitations to display her paintings in prominent places like New York and Paris. Emma's heart pounded with excitement and trepidation as she started this new phase of her artistic journey.

Her first significant exhibition took place in a prestigious New York City gallery. A group of art lovers, collectors, and prominent figures in the art world greeted Emma as she walked inside the gallery. As everyone excitedly awaited the debut of her most recent works, the atmosphere was electric with expectation.

As Emma approached the podium to give a speech on her artistic journey and the importance of optimism in her life and art, the room became silent. Her remarks captivated the audience, and paid close attention to everything she said. They were fascinated by Emma's honesty and vulnerability, which shined through.

The crowd erupted in wonder when the curtains were drawn to unveil Emma's latest collection. Her artwork displayed a command of technique, a breadth of feeling, and a singular capacity to concretize the essence of hope. The spectators were lured into a universe where optimism was tangible and vibrant because each brushstroke appeared to shine with vitality.

Art critics gave the exhibition glowing reviews, praising Emma's masterful use of color, her capacity to create feeling, and her profound storytelling through art. Emma's paintings saw a sharp increase in demand as a result of collectors' fascination with the unadulterated beauty and underlying message of each piece.

Her works were in high demand from collectors who appreciated their aesthetic value and the more profound inspiration and meaning they provided. Emma's artwork was no longer something to be appreciated; instead, it had become beloved reminders of human spirit-lifting power that would adorn the walls of people's homes, workplaces, and public places.

Despite her increasing success, Emma never wavered in her commitment to using art to inspire optimism. By donating a portion of her artwork's sales to organizations offering therapeutic and art-educational programs to impoverished communities, she used her newfound platform to spread awareness and support for causes that shared her ideals.

As Emma's work gained popularity, she started to support up-and-coming artists by using her position to open doors and provide platforms for undiscovered talent. She organized shows that highlighted promising young artists, promoted diversity, and honored the many different artistic voices that contributed to the fabric of the art world.

Despite her success, Emma always remembered the value of her neighborhood and the individuals who had helped her from the start. She created scholarships for budding artists, providing them with resources and mentorship programs to develop their skills and enable them to follow their artistic goals.

Emma's influence went far beyond art through her exhibitions, partnerships, and charitable endeavors. Her work became a symbol of hope, encouraging people from all walks of life to have faith in their creative abilities and harness the strength of optimism in their lives.

Emma understood as she reflected on her artistic career that the number of shows, awards, or sales was not the only metric of success. What mattered were the intense bonds she had created, the lives she had impacted, and the hope she had given others.

Emma kept painting, pouring her heart and soul into each canvas and injecting hope into her work. She constantly reminded herself and the rest of the world that, even in the most hopeless circumstances, hope could be found, fostered, and shared via the universal language of art.

The Emma Center for the Arts Fosters Creativity

Emma felt tremendous gratitude for the people who had supported her throughout her journey as her art gained prominence and her impact grew. She was aware of her desire to give back and establish an environment in which others might explore their creative potential and find peace in the transforming qualities of art. She, therefore, started a new project: creating a community art center.

Emma's goal was to renovate the outdated, run-down art studio she had found in her neighborhood and turn it into a thriving center for creative expression. The art studio started to change thanks to volunteers, regional craftspeople, and kind donations. The floors were polished, the walls were patched, and the room had an air of expectation.

Emma's excitement was out of control as the renovations got closer to being finished. The art center was more than simply a building; it stood for a haven of creativity and hope, a place where people of all ages and backgrounds could gather, pursue their artistic talents, and find inspiration in a welcoming environment.

The art center was excitedly buzzing on the day of the inaugural ceremony. People of various ages and backgrounds gathered, their eyes wide with intrigue and enthusiasm. Emma's voice was filled with emotion as she spoke about her idea for the art center while standing in front of the audience.

Emma proclaimed, "This is a place where creativity knows no bounds, where the power of art can heal, inspire, and unite people." "I hope this art center will act as a lighthouse of hope, a haven for those in need of comfort, and a spark for both individual and societal transformation."

The doors were thrown open, and the audience poured inside to peruse the numerous exhibits. Studios featuring easels, paintings, and brushes welcomed aspiring painters to let their imaginations run wild. Local artists had a place to display their works and tell their experiences in a gallery environment that featured their work.

The center provided classes and workshops in various disciplines, including sculpture, photography, mixed media, and traditional art forms. Locally accomplished artists who shared Emma's passion for encouraging creativity and fostering hope through art taught these sessions.

The art center started to bustle with activity as the days evolved into weeks. Children and seniors of all ages flocked to the center to partake in classes, see exhibitions, or relax in the tranquil setting. Laughter brushes on the canvas, and the buzz of creative energy fills the room.

Emma worked hard to create a sense of belonging at the art center. She planned art therapy sessions for people with various difficulties, giving them a secure environment to express themselves and find healing through art. In order to make art activities accessible to underprivileged people, the art center also worked with nearby schools and community organizations. This ensured that everyone could express their creativity.

The art center had a significant effect—individuals who had never considered themselves artists uncovered untapped abilities and a fresh passion.

The art center developed into a place where people could pursue their artistic ambitions, where friendships could grow among joint creative endeavors, and where dreams could come true.

One specific tale had a profound impact on Emma. One day, Lily, a young woman struggling with depression, entered the art center. Lily was initially reserved and found comfort in her artistic endeavors. She experienced a sense of relief with each brushstroke, a method to express her feelings and see a glimmer of hope.

Lily's confidence increased thanks to the encouragement and direction of the art center's instructors, and her artwork developed into a potent form of self-expression. Visitors were drawn in by her colorful, moving paintings, and before long, she was showing her work alongside works by well-known artists.

Lily's journey parallels Emma's as they learn art can heal, inspire, and unite people. Lily, previously trapped in the depths of misery, discovered her voice and purpose through painting while Emma watched with pride.

The flourishing art center rose to prominence as a source of inspiration and proof of the healing potential of creativity. People whose lives had been impacted by the art center sent Emma gratitude, sharing tales of their personal development, rekindled passion, and discovered purpose.

Emma once noticed an older woman sitting by herself in the corner of the art gallery and looking at a picture with tear-filled eyes. Emma approached her and kindly inquired about her needs. The woman, Margaret, said the artwork made her think of her late husband, an enthusiastic painter who had passed away years earlier.

Margaret's tale moved Emma, so she invited her to exhibit her husband's work in a special exhibition for the public. The occasion evolved into celebrating love, creativity, and Margaret's husband's enduring legacy.

During the exhibition, Emma stood amidst the colorful pieces of art and the pleasant conversation. She realized that her aim of using art to spread hope had succeeded beyond her wildest dreams. The art center had developed into a physical illustration of the creative force and the human spirit's capacity for resiliency.

The art center left a lasting effect beyond its actual presence. Each person who entered its doors felt like they had a spark kindled inside them, inspiring them to see their artistic potential and hold onto hope even in the most challenging circumstances.

The art center thrived in the following years, inspiring innumerable artists, kindling imaginations, and developing a sense of community. Emma's dream had come true, touching people's spirits, igniting their creativity, and leaving a lasting legacy of hope via art in the minds and hearts of anyone who had the privilege of experiencing it.

"The Hub"

As the art center's reputation grew, artists started swarming near and far to its doors. While aspiring artists discovered a loving group where they could grow and learn, established artists acknowledged the encouraging atmosphere and camaraderie permeating the space.

The art center became a creative hotspot humming with activity and overflowing with motivation. As they worked together on projects and pushed one another to new heights, artists from all genres and backgrounds exchanged knowledge and techniques. The unfettered flow of ideas fostered a culture of continuous learning and exploration.

Emma assumed the roles of mentor and guide because she was the art center's creator and primary motivator. She organized master courses and workshops and invited well-known artists to share their knowledge with the neighborhood. The art center evolved into an educational location where artists could hone their craft, explore new mediums, and push the limits of their creativity.

David was one such artist who came to the art center with a strong enthusiasm for sculpture. Although it was clear that he had talent, he lacked self-assurance and found it difficult to express himself. When Emma saw his potential, she took him under her wing and gave him advice and support.

Emma and David started a path of artistic exploration together. They investigated various sculpture techniques, examined the works of well-known sculptors, and had stimulating discussions on art and its influence on society. Through Emma's guidance, David's sculptures started to take on a style that mirrored his life experiences and goals.

The art center evolved into a venue for artists to display their creations and achieve recognition. Regular art shows were arranged to display the community's array of talents. The novelty and depth of the paintings on display attracted art fans, collectors, and critics to these exhibitions.

In one of these exhibitions, Maya, a young artist, displayed her work. Maya had experienced many difficulties but found comfort and healing in her creativity. Her paintings reflected her path of overcoming adversity by showing periods of vulnerability, strength, and resiliency.

Visitors were struck by the real emotion and honesty Maya expressed through her brushstrokes as her art adorned the walls of the art center. Critics acclaimed her for her ability to arouse strong emotions in the viewer, and collectors swooped in to buy her paintings after seeing the enormous talent and promise in them.

Within the community of the art center, the success of artists like Maya, David, and several others had a cascading impact. With their work being displayed in galleries, museums, and public places, artists started to achieve notoriety outside the boundaries of the art center. The art center gained a reputation as a hub for innovation and creativity, and its artists were in demand for commissions, team projects, and public art initiatives.

But despite the recognition and success, the art center never forgot its primary goal—to use art to bring about constructive change. Emma and the local artists realized art could evoke emotion, foster empathy, and spur societal change.

Collaborative projects addressed topics including social justice, mental health awareness, and environmental preservation. Together, artists produced compelling installations, murals, and performances that questioned social conventions and provoked discussions.

One of these initiatives involves converting a run-down neighborhood park into a bright, all-encompassing art piece. The community came together to give the area new life and gave their time, talents, and resources. A kaleidoscope of color and inventiveness emerged, bearing witness to the neighborhood's resiliency and shared goals.

The renovated park attracted tourists far and wide as a sign of renewal and hope. It was more than simply a physical location; it was a symbol of the ability of art to influence people's lives and the conviction that even the most forgotten areas of society might benefit from the creative process.

The art center kept thriving, and its influence went beyond the art world. The network of like-minded people who thought that art might improve the world it nurtured evolved into a support system. To inspire and empower the next generation, artists became mentors to aspiring artists, imparting their wisdom, experiences, and resources.

Emma was proud to see how the art center sparked societal change, individual development, and neighborhood improvement. It had exceeded her wildest expectations as a venue for creative expression and a catalyst for progress.

Even amid the art center's triumph, Emma never lost sight of her difficulties. She maintained her modesty, always ready to listen and advise anyone who needed it. Her generosity and commitment to the neighborhood inspired everyone who contacted her.

The influence of the art center grew over the years. It attracted creators, enthusiasts, and curious minds worldwide as a light of inspiration and hope. The art center's standing as a catalyst for social transformation was cemented by the widespread recognition of the facility as a transforming setting.

Emma's dream had come true: a vibrant artistic community bound by a shared conviction about the transformative power of art. She couldn't help but feel profound gratitude for the fantastic adventure she had taken as she surveyed the bustling art center.

The collective spirit of resiliency, creativity, and hope that emanated from within the walls of the art center served as its legacy rather than merely the building itself or the artworks it held. One brushstroke at a time, the art center's influence would continue molding people's lives, stimulating thought, and leaving a lasting mark on the globe.

Trying Out Different Shades Of Hope

With a brush in her hand, Emma stood before her easel, thinking about her upcoming creative project. The art center had developed into a hive of creative activity, a gathering place for creatives from all walks of life. It served as a tribute to both the transforming potential of art and the strength of hope.

Emma had seen innumerable tales of tenacity and success within the walls of the art center over the years. She had witnessed the power of art to heal, arouse emotion, and unite people. But she realized in her heart that she still had a long way to go in her career as an artist.

Emma had always been drawn to the brilliant color combinations because of the way they sang and danced on the canvas, communicating feelings that language could never explain. She mastered several painting methods and produced stunning landscapes, portraits, and abstract pieces. However, she yearned for more as she longed to push the limits of her creativity and investigate new artistic possibilities.

Emma once noticed a collection of sculpting supplies while browsing the racks of a nearby art supply store. She picked up a slab of clay and ran her fingertips over its smooth surface, intrigued by the possibilities before her. Her excitement grew, and she realized sculpting was the key to her upcoming artistic endeavors.

Emma enrolled in sculpting workshops, eager to study the nuances of this ancient art form, with a newfound feeling of purpose. She plunged into the world of three-dimensional creativity while being guided by an expert sculptor, molding and sculpting clay with her hands. The tactile element of sculpting allowed her to immerse herself in the process, which was very different from painting.

Emma experienced a renewed sense of independence as her sculptures took shape. She infused life into her works of art with each movement of her fingers, rendering in clay the very soul of her subjects. She carved strong, resilient, and unwaveringly hopeful characters. Her actions appeared to be controlled by an invisible force that channeled the feelings she was experiencing.

Emma's particular haven and place of growth and exploration became the art center. She experimented with many methods and mediums for endless hours in the studio. She worked with clay and mixed colors and believed art could change people. Her artwork evolved into a mirror of her journey and a demonstration of how hope is ever-evolving.

As word of Emma's sculpting abilities circulated among the art world, people started noticing her works. Art lovers were stunned by the emotional intricacy and depth of her creations. She received accolades from critics for depicting the complexities of the human experience in her sculptures, which they said captured the spirit of hope.

Despite the praise and admiration, Emma maintained her sense of reality. She realized that her artistic journey wasn't about recognition or outside approval. It was a private and individualized journey—a look for the myriad nuances of hope within her spirit.

Emma started working on a series of sculptures that examined the various dimensions of hope after being inspired by the stories she had heard at the art center. She carved figures reaching upward, their outstretched arms signifying unbounded ambitions. She created elaborate mosaics by joining disparate pieces of brokenness to form something lovely and complete. Each sculpture recounted a unique tale of triumph over hardship and the emergence of light from darkness.

Emma's sculptures were shown in the art center, drawing tourists from all over. People gazed intently at each piece as they stood in wonder, entranced by the feelings the clay was emitting. Emma's sculptures moved people, sparked discussions, and made people think about their travels and find comfort in the beauty of hope.

One specific sculpture, "Eternal Spring," represented tenacity and renewal. The image showed a figure emerging from a cocoon as its wings spread out in a triumphant manifestation of transformation. The sculpture struck a powerful chord with those who had endured trials and setbacks, reminding them that hope might lead them to a better future even amid the most dire circumstances.

Emma continued to experiment with other media once she finished sculpting. She experimented with mixed media, fusing painting, sculpture, and other forms of art to produce three-dimensional works that defied classification. Installations were an experimental medium she used to immerse visitors in a realm of color, sound, and feeling. Her creations connected various artistic mediums, encouraging viewers to view hope from various angles.

Emma saw something extraordinary within the art center as she continued pushing her creativity's boundaries. Artists who had previously limited their work to painting or sculpture started experimenting with new media. The atmosphere buzzed with creative energy as artists worked on projects, shared ideas, and challenged one another to reach new heights.

The art center had developed into a thriving tapestry of artistic expression, symbolizing creativity's capacity for transformation. It was a location where optimism grew, artists dug deep inside themselves, and the locals found comfort and motivation.

Emma couldn't help but be deeply grateful as she reflected on her adventure. She developed her artistic skills at the art center, which also served as a catalyst for development and change within the creative community. By experimenting with various media, Emma has inspired people to be curious and brave by pushing them to leave their comfort zones and embrace the uncharted.

Emma had a wave of emotions as she stood in the middle of the art center, surrounded by the results of her artistic exploration. The path had not always been simple; there had been times when I felt insecure, impatient, and uncertain. But despite it all, she had come to understand the limitless reservoir of optimism she possessed and had seen the transformative power of art.

Emma's artistic development was evidence of hope's flexible nature. It served as a reminder that while hope may seem static at times, it is a living, dynamic energy that can be expressed in many different ways. Emma had created a tapestry of optimism via her paintings, sculptures, and mixed-media works that touched hearts, stimulated thought, and made a lasting impression on the world.

Emma's artistic development developed as the years went by. She had experimented with several mediums, broadened her creative horizons, and established a thriving art center that inspired and promoted a sense of community. Emma's heart was torn as she wondered, "What was the true nature of hope" amid the flurry of achievement and acclaim?

She considered this while seated in front of her easel, her palette overflowing with brilliant colors. Emma dipped her brush into a basin of cerulean blue paint and began painting. A serene ocean at dusk was shown on the canvas with broad brushstrokes. She stood back to admire her work but couldn't shake the feeling that something was wrong.

Emma understood that, like the ocean, optimism was not limited to a single color. It was a rainbow of feelings, encounters, and opportunities. It was the fiery red of steadfastness, the gentle pink of compassion, the golden yellow of resilience, and the vivid orange of daybreak. It was a harmonious symphony of hues that danced in perfect harmony.

After gaining this new insight, Emma started a series of paintings examining hope's complex nature. Each image became a doorway into a distinct facet of the human experience, a representation in pictures of the complex feelings that hope inspired. She captured the warmth and happiness of shared times in her paintings of happy situations. She depicted images of sadness while portraying the grit and resiliency that were evident even in the most trying circumstances.

One specific artwork, titled "The Mosaic of Hope," developed to become the collection's focal point. It included a mosaic of numerous tiny pieces, each distinctive color, shape, and texture. While some parts were jagged and flawed, others were polished and smooth. But when combined, they created an incredible work of art that exemplified the variety and interconnection of human experiences.

The depth and emotion that Emma's paintings captured as they were on display caught the attention of spectators. People who looked at the painting experienced an emotional reaction as the colors appeared to jump off the canvas. As they admired Emma's crafts, people from all walks of life found comfort, inspiration, and optimism.

However, Emma's journey was about more than simply the paintings. It was all about the human connection and how her artwork affected other people's lives. She saw individuals sobbing happily, hugging one another during vulnerable times, and rediscovering their resiliency. Emma discovered the immense potential she possessed to touch hearts and change lives via her art.

Emma's paintings gained more and more popularity over time. Despite the pressure from galleries and art buyers to show her work, she stayed faithful to her goals. For artists from all walks of life, the art center she had founded became a haven where they could find assistance, inspiration and express their visions of hope freely.

Emma's influence went well beyond just her artistic accomplishments. She had sparked a spark in others, inspiring them to unleash their creativity and embrace the rainbow of optimism they already possessed. The art center evolved into a symbol of the capacity of art and the human spirit to transcend.

Emma never forgot about her journey, even in the thick of praise and accomplishment. She kept painting because of her unquenchable curiosity and undying faith in the ability of art to enlighten the world. She painted with a deep appreciation, aware that she had been given a gift: the capacity to inspire hope and change lives via her work.

Emma realized that hope was more than an idea or a transitory feeling as she reflected on her life's work. It was a lifetime endeavor, a constant force that directed her brush, stoked her imagination, and kept her in touch with the outside world. She would leave behind more than just a collection of paintings—she would also go a lasting tribute to the strength of optimism.

Emma thus carried on painting. She embraced the rainbow of feelings, encounters, and opportunities that characterized hope with each stroke. Knowing that each color in life's spectrum has a special meaning, she accepted the highs and lows, the pleasures and the sorrows.

Emma understood that her journey was far from over as she shared her creativity with the world. She had learned that hope was a constant thread that ran through every instant of existence rather than an end in itself. The warmth warmed the coldest hearts, the steadfast faith in a better tomorrow, and the brightness shone into the deepest crevices.

Through the paintings Emma left behind, the art center she established, and the lives she impacted, her narrative would continue to be told. But more than anything, it would endure in the hearts of those who had experienced the healing power of hope through her creations.

The tradition of optimism so carried on, creating a vibrant tapestry that will inspire future generations.

www.ingramcontent.com/pod-product-compliance
Lightning Source LLC
Chambersburg PA
CBHW072215290526
45794CB00004B/1758